SEEN THE NEW NOTICE BOARD?

COLLECTED and COMPILED
BY

LES YEOMAN
PAUL ALLINGTON
STEVE GILLARD
&
NATASHA THOMPSON

IDEAS UNLIMITED (PUBLISHING)

Published by:

Ideas Unlimited (Publishing)

P.O. Box 125, Portsmouth
Hampshire PO1 4PP

©1995 **Ideas Unlimited (Publishing)**

Les Yeoman
Paul Allington
Steve Gillard

ISBN I 871964180

Illustrations by Willy Sanker

Printed and bound in Great Britain

INTRODUCTION

It was only a short while since the last Notice Board Book was published. And such is the popularity of the book it is a must that another version be produced. The office and notice boards seem to continue to bulge with a plentiful supply of material. Are our jobs so boring or mundane that we have nothing better to do with our time or is it that we really are a jolly bunch of office workers who sincerely enjoy taking the mickey out of each other and ourselves - or our bosses in many instances. Do they really mind, do we really care!

The examples contained herein are proof that the British humour has not changed despite recession, redundancy and the difficulties of life under Tory government!

We continue to playfully ridicule each other including ourselves because without humour on a daily basis and, particularly, in an office environment life really would be rather boring and mundane. Mirth, merriment, jollification on a regular basis is the meaning of life, the very thing the doctor did prescribe but which the NHS did not have to pay for.

In producing the many versions of material for the notice boards within the many offices the anonymous authors have shown great perception, foresight and insight into the problems and difficulties of office life or, indeed, any building which contains, captives and harbours human beings removing them from the green fields and fresh air.
It is refreshing and stimulating, relieves the monotony, releases the mind when reading the routine office memo on the notice board and then to notice a piece of literary art penned or typed or drawn and created whilst ones mind wanders at the desk or keyboard - and to be paid for it as well!!

In this version of "SEEN THE NEW NOTICE BOARD?" it is hoped not to offend with the more risque of material but to genuinely amuse and even encourage this increasingly funny form of legal graffiti.

LES P. YEOMAN
Plymouth 1995

INTRODUCTION

I would have liked to have jotted down something deep and meaningful about the literacy contribution that these pages represent. I would like to share wacky experiences with you, the reader, of the way these missives were collected. I would like to think these pages in some way form a crazy comfort by way of lightening dark moments. The truth is there really isn't anything deep and meaningful - just sharp and biting wit. There were no wacky doings surrounding the acquisition of the pages - just a mate saying 'Have you seen this?'

They do however, lighten dark moments and cause (in some less inhibited persons) paroxysms of laughter with bodies rolling uncontrollably around the floor. The beauty of it all is that we are still able to laugh in the face of those everyday things that threaten us. Something terrible happens and we say 'oh that's bad, let's make a joke of it'.

The one thing that is shared universally is laughter - the feel-good factor. While I would take my hat off (if I wore one) to all those Mr and Mrs Anonymous that penned the pages herein, the one guy I admire the most is the one from way-back-when that said 'Hey, I've just thought of something that everyone can have a go at and it makes you feel so much better - I think I'm going to call it 'laughing', you see what you do is, you curl your lips at the corners...like this, look...and then...'

Paul Allington
Lowestoft 1995

It is not often that an author spends more time writing the introduction and acknowledgments than writing the book itself, but then I am no author, merely a collector. It therefore gives me great pleasure in sharing over twenty years of collecting notice board humour with you and my fellow contributors, and hope that you enjoy "SEEN THE NEW NOTICE BOARD?" as much as I have. If any of these jokes offend or shock you in any way, then I ofer apologies, and add in the words of a friend of mine "TOUGH!".

Stephen Gillard
Maidstone 1995

We wish to convey our gratitude to everyone involved with this project in whatever capacity. Our special thanks goes to Les Yeoman, Stephen Gillard and Paul Allington for their collection of the material which they have painstakenly collected over a number of years, and Natasha Thomson for the collation of the additional material included in the book.

We are grateful to Bob Crabtree and John Hill for their very clever flow charts intended to help us out of those sticky situations.

A final thanks goes to our very talented cartoonist Willy Sanker for his contribution, without which this book would have been meaningless to those too lazy to read.

The Publishers.

ACKNOWLEDGEMENTS

Where does all this material keep coming from? Why does one keep it? You only have to look on the many notice boards around the offices and factory floors to answer the first question.
As to why we keep it - because it is intrinsically funny and as you move from job to job you never know when it might come in handy, when it might be very relevant and whether it will add a touch of humour to another audience.

It is to these unknown artists and authors that we must acknowledge our thanks and gratitude for without them where would we be!

Equally, thanks to my wife Susan and daughter Rachel for their humour, support and for encouraging me to go ahead with publishing this graffiti in order that the multitudes can share and appreciate this wonderful collection.

Les P. Yeoman
Plymouth 1995

It has been one of my ambitions for many years to have my collection of notice board humour published. That ambition has now been realised thanks to Brian Lee-Blackmore and "HAVE YOU SEEN THE NOTICE BOARD?" which inspired me to finally submit my collection for publication. I would like to thank the unknown authors of these works of public domain literature and my family, friends and acquaintances for the material they supplied and thanks also to Jobsworths everywhere especially at 'Charley One".

Stephen Gillard
Maidstone 1995

Mostly the works collected are scraps of paper that were handed to me, sent to me, faxed to me, pinned up in front of me, served to with fish and chips, laying in dentists and doctors waiting rooms, uncovered in lofts, magazine racks, box files, bins, baskets, basins and other places that things collect. Whoever was responsible for authorising said items a big hearty thanks and a hey-nonny-nonny to some of those that helped me acquire them - Bill, Mike, Brian, Tiny, Wayne, Andy, Matt, Max, Mum, Dad, and Sue.

In fact, if you take the initials of the people above, put them in reverse and add an A in-between every two letter, say it in a Swedish accent with a tulip in your ear and a wistful look edging across your face, you get a word that just creases me up every time.

Paul Allington
Lowestoff 1995.

FOR SERVICE

RING BELL
WHISTLE
SHOUT
SCREAM
WHIMPER
BEG
THREATEN
GROVEL
WHINE

IF NONE OF THE
ABOVE WORKS,

GO AWAY

TO THE VISITOR

CIGARETTE SMOKE IS THE RESIDUE OF YOUR
PLEASURE.
IT PERMEATES THE AIR AND PUTREFIES MY HAIR
AND CLOTHES NOT TO MENTION MY LUNGS.

THIS TAKES PLACE WITHOUT MY CONSENT.
I HAVE A PLEASURE ALSO.
I LIKE A CAN OR TWO OF FOSTERS BEER
NOW AND THEN.

THE RESIDUE FROM MY PLEASURE IS URINE.
WOULD YOU BE ANNOYED IF I STOOD ON A
CHAIR AND PISSED ON YOUR CLOTHES
WITHOUT YOUR CONSENT?

WHY BEER IS BETTER THAN WOMEN

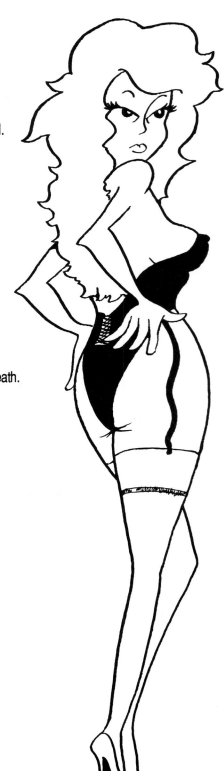

1. You can enjoy beer all month long.

2. Beer stains wash out.

3. You don't have to wine and dine beer.

4. Your beer will always wait patiently for you in your car while you play football.

5. When your beer goes flat you toss it out.

6. Beer is never late.

7. Hangovers go away.

8. A beer doesn't get jealous if you grab another one.

9. Beer labels come off without a fight.

10. When you go into a bar you know you can always pick up a beer.

11. Beer never has a headache.

12. A beer won't be upset if you come home and have another beer on your breath.

13. If you pour a beer right, you always get good head.

14. You can have more than one beer a night and not feel guilty.

15. A beer always goes down easily.

16. You can share a beer with your friends.

17. You always know you're the first one to pop a beer.

18. The beer is always wet.

19. A beer doesn't demand equality.

20. You can have a beer in public.

21. A beer doesn't care when you come home.

22. A frigid beer is a good beer.

23. You don't have to wash a beer to make it taste good.

24. If you change beer you don't have to pay alimony.

25. A beer doesn't complain about your beer gut.

THOUGHT FOR TODAY

Now look at the bottom left hand letter as an exclamation mark.

LOO-DILEMMA

No.9 in the Series:
a Flowcharting Guide to Life

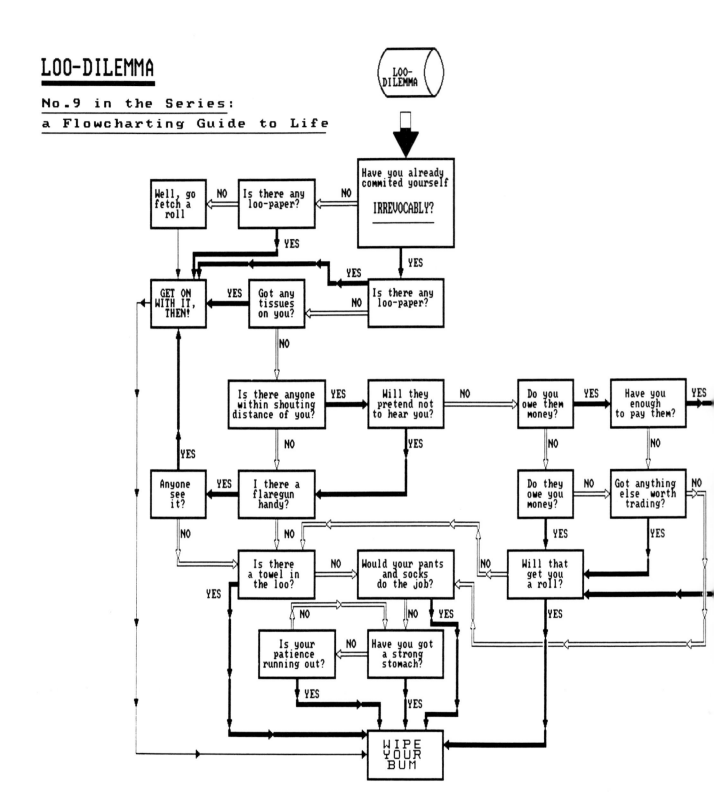

Character Analysis

Study the following carefully and see which applies to you:

1. Excitable type........... Pant's twisted, can't find the hole, tears his pants in a temper.

2. Sociable type........... Joins his friends to piss whether he wants to or not, says it costs him nothing. Can't piss if anyone is watching him.

3. Timid type............... Pretends to piss and sneaks back later.

4. Noisy type............... Whistles loudly-peeps over the partition to look at other blokes tools.

5. Indifferent type.......... Urinal being full - pisses in sink.

6. Clever type.............. Pisses without holding tool. Shows off by adjusting tie at same time.

7. Frivolous type........... Plays the stream up, down and across-tries to piss on flies as they pass to and fro.

8. Absent type.............. Opens vest, takes out tie and pisses himself.

9. Worried type............. Makes furtive examination of tool without pissing.

10. Disgruntled type........ Stands for a while, grunts, farts and walks out muttering.

11. Personality type......... Tells jokes while pissing. Shakes off drops with great flourish.

12. Sneaky type............. Drops a silent fart while pissing, sniffs and looks at bloke in next cubicle.

13. Sloppy type............. Pisses down trousers into shoes, walks out with fly-hole open and adjusts testicles in street.

14. Learned type............ Reads books or papers while pissing.

15. Childish type............ Gazes down at bottom of urinal whilst pissing to watch the bubbles.

16. Vain type................. Unfastens five buttons when he knows one would do.

17. Strong type.............. Bangs tool on side of urinal to knock drops off.

18. Unlucky type............ Tries to fart-shits himself and finds he can't piss.

DER FUKKENGRETTRUKKEN

A useful little glossary of English/German motoring terms which may come in useful next time your motor becomes wedged beneath a fukken great juggernaut.

Speedometer	Der Egobooster und Linenshooter.
Puncture	Die Phlattmitt Bludyfuckken.
Learner	Die Twatten mit Elplatz.
Estatecar	Der Baggeroom fur schaggink inauto.
Windscreen Wiper	Der flippenflappen Mukkenschpredder.
Foot Brake	Der Edbangeron Vindskreen.
Gear Lever	Biggenstikken fur Kangeroohoppen.
Breathalyser	Die Puffinbag fur Pisterarsen.
Headlights	Das Dippendont Dazl-u-Basted.
Exhaust Fumes	Der Kofen und Schpitternpoluter.
Highway Code	Der Wipen fur Aarsen.
Fog Warning	Die Puttenleg Downen und Fukkit.
Traffic Jam	Die Bluddenfukkit Dammundblast.
Backfire	Der Lowden Bangen Mekkenjumppen.
Juggernaut	Der Fukkengrett Trukken.
Accident	Der Bleedinmess.
Near Accident	Der Fukken Near Schittenselfen.
Garage	Der Heiway Robberung.
Double White Lines	Overtaken und Krunchen.

Our thanks to bi-linguist K. Thomas of Snetterton Mudflaps, for filling us in on this information.

GET DOWN SHEP!

" HE LIKES YOU! "

Chief Recipe For Banana Bread

Ingredients

Two laughing eyes
Two loving arms
Two well shaped legs
Two firm milk containers
One fur mixing bowl
One long banana
Two large walnuts

Method

1. Look into the laughing eyes.

2. Fold into the loving arms.

3. Spread well shaped legs.

4. Squeeze & massage milk containers very gently
   until fur lined mixing bowl is greased.
   Check frequently with middle finger.

5. Add banana and gently work in and out until well creamed.

6. Cover with nuts and sigh with relief.

7. Bread is done when banana is soft.

8. Be sure to wash utensils & don't lick bowl.

9. Note If bread starts to rise, leave room immediately.

Panties

A young man wished to purchase a gift for his new sweetheart's birthday and as they had not been dating very long, after careful consideration, he decided a pair of gloves would strike the right note. Romantic but not too personal. Accompanied by his sweetheart's younger sister, he went to Sears and bought a pair of gloves. The younger sister purchased a pair of panties for herself. During the wrapping, the clerk mixed up the items and the sister got the gloves, and the sweetheart got the panties. Without checking the contents, he sealed the package and mailed it to his sweetheart along with this note:

Darling,

I chose these because I noticed that you are not in the habit of wearing any when we go out in the evening. If it had not been for your sister, I would have chosen the long ones with buttons, but she wears short ones which are easy to remove.

These are a delicate shade, but the lady I bought them from showed me the pair she was wearing for the past weeks, and they were hardly soiled. I had her try yours on and she looked smart.

I wish I was there to put them on for you the first time, as no doubt other hands will come in contact with them before I have a chance to see you again.

When you take them off, remember to blow in them before putting them away as they will be a little damp from wearing. Just think how many times I will kiss them during the coming year.

I hope you will wear them Friday night.

All My Love,

Edward.

P.S. The latest style is to wear them folded down with a little fur showing.

MEN USED TO DREAM ABOUT THEM - NOW WOMEN DO, TOO.

YES, WE'RE TALKING...

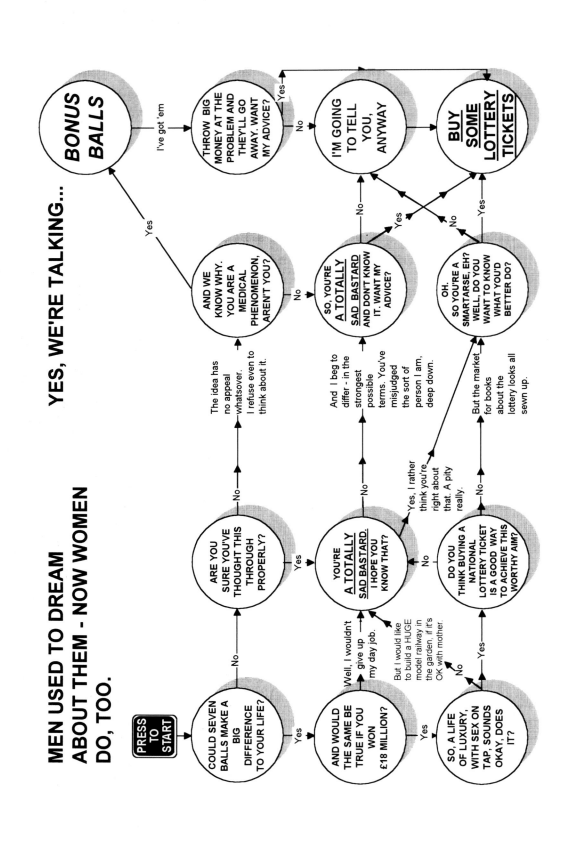

££££££££££££££££££££££££££££££

Being a Millionaire isn't everything.
It may give you a roof over your head.
It may give you power,
Food in your
stomach,
Provide
health care,
A face lift
Friends
Material
things to
amuse you
Pleasures
of the flesh
But can it give
you happiness?

YES!

I'm fine thank you

There is nothing the matter with me,
I'm as healthy as I can be.
I have arthritis in both my knees
And when I talk, I talk with a wheeze.
My pulse is weak, and my blood is thin,
But I'm awfully well for the shape I'm in.

Arch supports I have for my feet,
Or I wouldn't be able to be on the street.
Sleep is denied me night after night,
But every morning I find I'm alright.
My memory is failing, my head's in a spin
But I'm awfully well for the shape I'm in.

How do I know that my youth is all spent?
Well my Get up and go has got up and went.
But I really don't mind when I think with a grin,
Of all the grand places my Get up has bin.

Old age is golden I've heard it said
But, sometimes I wonder as I get into bed.
With my ears in the drawer, my teeth in a cup,
My eyes on the table until I wake up.
Ere sleep overtakes me, I say to myself,
Is there anything else I could lay on the shelf?

I get up each morning and dust off my wits
And pick up the paper and read the Obits
If my name is still missing I know I'm not dead,
So I have a good breakfast and go back to bed.

ANON.

A ROUND TUIT

....

At long last we have a sufficient quantity for each of you to have your own. These tuits have been hard to come by, especially the round ones. This is an indispensable item. It will help you become a much more efficient worker. For years we have heard people say: "I'll do this as soon as I get a round tuit". Now that you have a round tuit of your own, many things that have been needing to be accomplished will get done.....

a round tuit a round tuit a round tuit a round tuit a round tuit a round tuit a round tuit a round tuit a round tuit a round tuit a round tuit a round tuit a round tuit a round tuit

Re - additional training for all staff

A) It is now , and always has been, the policy of this company to assure its employees are well trained. Through our "SPECIAL HIGH INTENSITY TRAINING' programme. S.H.I.T. for short. We have given our employees more S.H.I.T. than any other company in the area.
If any employee feels that he or she does not receive enough S.H.I.T. on the job, or that he or she could advance to another position by taking more S.H.I.T. Please see your immediate supervisor.

B) If you graduate to the top of this list by taking all the S.H.I.T. that is given to you, you can then qualify for our supervisors programme "COMPLETE RESPONSIBILITY ACTION PROGRAMME" C.R.A.P. For short.
So to become a member of our management team, simply take all the S.H.I.T. you can, and then with all the additional C.R.A.P. you receive you will soon reach the top. Any employee who has the initiative and drive to take both S.H.I.T. and C.R.A.P. will soon become one of the elite.

C) For a limited period only, the company is offering all employees the chance to try for our latest scheme 'ADVANCED SUPERVISORY STAFF HELPING OUR LOYAL EMPLOYEES' A.S.S.H.O.L.E. for short.
So work hard and you will find that the more S.H.I.T. you take and the more C.R.A.P. you can handle, you will qualify as an A.S.S.H.O.L.E. for sure.

THE COMPANY MOTTO

BE FLEXIBLE!

This is his Life

From 20 to 30 - If a man lives right
               It's once in the morning & twice at night
From 30 to 40 - If he still lives right
               He misses a morning & sometimes at night
From 40 to 50 - It's just now and then
From 50 to 60 - It's God knows when
From 60 to 70 - If he's still inclined -

But don't let him kid you
It's still in his mind.
His sporting days are over
His little light is out -
What used to be his sex appeal
Is now his water spout
It used to be embarrassing
To make the thing behave
For nearly every morning
It stood and watched him shave
But now it's getting older
It sure gives him the blues
To have it dangling down his legs
And watch him clean his shoes.

Out of the Gloom a
voice said unto me
"Smile and be happy;
things could be worse"

So I smiled and was
happy
and behold, things did
get worse!

I'm Tired

Yes I'm tired. For several years I've been blaming it on middle age, poor blood, lack of vitamins, air pollution, saccharin, obesity, dieting, under arm odour, yellow wax build up and another dozen maladies that make you wonder if life is worth living.

But I find out it isn't that.

I'm tired because I'm overworked.

The population of this country is 51 million and 21 million are retired. That leaves 30 million to do the work. There are 19 million in school. That leaves 11 million. Of this total 2 million are unemployed and 4 million are employed by the government. That leaves 5 million to do the work. One million are in the armed forces which leaves 4 million to do the work. From that total, 3 million are employed by County and Borough Councils, leaving 1 million people to do the work. There are 62,000 people in hospital and 937,998 people in prisons.

That leaves 2 people to do the work.

You and me.

And you are sitting on your arse reading this.

No wonder I'm bloody tired.

MY OBJECTIVE IS

To thoroughly analyse all new situations; anticipate problems prior to their occurring; have the answers to these problems ready; and move swiftly when called upon.

HOWEVER

When your'e up to your ass in alligators it is difficult to remind yourself that your initial objective was to drain the swamp.

HM Inspector of Taxes
Crown Building Windmill Road London SW3 5AA
Telephone (01998 376542)

District Inspector: Mr Spoons

My reference:	Your reference:	Date: As postmark

Dear Sir
INCREASED TAX PAYMENT 1995/96

It has come to our notice that the only thing the Inland Revenue has not taxed is your willy.
This is due to the fact that 40% of the time it is hanging around unemployed.
30 % of the time it is pissed off, 20% of the time it is hard up and 10% of the time it is employed in total darkness.
Furthermore, it has two dependants, and they are both nuts.

Accordingly, after 5 April 1996 you will be taxed according to the size of your willy.
Use the Pecker Checker below to find out your liability for Todger Tax.

CIRCUMFERENCE
(inches)

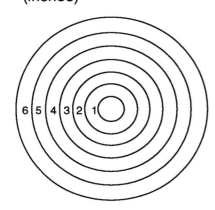

PECKER CHECKER
1. Length: place this letter on a table at groin height. Lay your willy along ruler (far right).
2. Circumference: cut out the circles (left) starting with the smallest until your willy just fits through.
3. Cross-reference the length and circumference on the chart (right) to find your todger tax rating.

Grade A: Nuisance Tax.........£50p.a.
Grade B: Privilege Tax........£100p.a.
Grade C: Pole Tax..............£150p.a.
Grade D: Luxury Tax...........£200p.a.

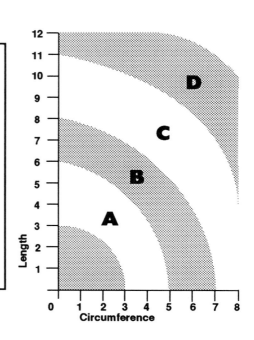

We should point out that calculations are only valid when your willy is fully extended.
The tax will be subject to a reduction of 15% for personal allowances.

Please note that anyone smaller than Grade A is eligible for a refund.
Males with a willy in excess of Grade D should file a special claim under 'Capital Gains'.

As we have found that this is the only occasion in which men are willing to pay more tax than would actually be due, we will be contacting you again in the near future to arrange for an Inspector to visit, in order to verify your tax liability.

Yours Faithfully

H M Inspector of Taxes.

EVERY DAY OF MY LIFE I'M FORCED TO ADD ANOTHER NAME TO THE LIST OF PEOPLE WHO PISS ME OFF

PERMANENT LIST

_____
_____
_____
_____
_____
_____
_____
_____
_____
_____
_____

LIST FOR TODAY

_____
_____
_____
_____
_____
_____
_____
_____
_____
_____

THE RULES FOR **GOLF**

1. EACH PLAYER SHALL HAVE ONE CLUB AND TWO BALLS. THE OBJECT OF THE GAME IS TO GET INTO THE HOLE IN THE LEAST NUMBER OF STROKES.

2. PLAYERS SHALL AT ALL TIMES USE A COVER ON THEIR CLUBS. THIS IS PARTICULARLY IMPORTANT WHEN PLAYING AN UNKNOWN COURSE WITH A PRO. FAILURE TO OBSERVE THIS RULE MAY HAVE SERIOUS CONSEQUENCES AND DAMAGE THE CLUB RESULTING IN PROLONGED ABSENCE FROM THE GAME. WHEN PLAYING THE HOME GAME THIS RULE SHOULD BE OBSERVED FOR ILL EFFECTS MAY BE CAUSED TO THE HOLE, AFTER SOME MONTHS THE HOLE MAY BECOME INCREASINGLY DIFFICULT TO PLAY AND FINALLY MAY HAVE TO BE TAKEN OUT FOR A WHILE, WHILE EXCAVATIONS ARE CARRIED OUT.

3. A PLAYER SHOULD OCCASIONALLY GREASE HIS CLUB WHEN PLAYING A NEW COURSE.

4. A RED FLAG IN ANY HOLE INDICATES THAT THE HOLE SHOULD NOT BE PLAYED FOR A FEW DAYS.

5. A PLAYER MAKING AN APPROACH FROM THE BACK OF THE GREEN MUST TAKE CARE NOT TO LAND HIS CLUB IN THE BUNKER AT THE BACK OF THE HOLE.

6. PRACTICE SWINGS OF THE CLUB ARE NOT ALLOWED IN THE LADIES' DRESSING ROOM, AND TOWELS MUST NOT BE USED FOR WIPING THE BALLS AFTER HOLING OUT.

7. OLD BAGS ARE NOT ALLOWED.

8. IN THE INTEREST OF OTHERS, ALL PLAYERS SHALL TAKE CARE NOT TO ENLARGE THE HOLE UNDULY, HOLES INTO WHICH A PLAYER CAN INSERT HIS CLUB AND BOTH BALLS AT ONE TIME, SHALL BE TAKEN OUT OF USE.

9. LOOSE IMPLEMENTS AT THE FRONT OR REAR OF THE HOLE MAY BE REMOVED IF INTERFERING WITH PLAY, EXCEPT WHEN THE RED FLAG IS FLYING.

10. IF A PLAYER BECOMES ENTANGLED IN THE ROUGH HE MAY BE WITHDRAWN AND TAKE THE STROKE AGAIN.

11. IF TWO OR MORE PLAYERS WISH TO PLAY A HOLE AT THE SAME TIME, THE DISPUTE SHALL BE RESOLVED AS FOLLOWS: EACH PLAYER SHALL PLACE HIS CLUB AT THE TOP OF THE HOLE, MEASUREMENTS SHALL BE TAKEN AND THE PLAYER WHOSE BALLS ARE FURTHERMOST FROM THE HOLE SHALL BE ALLOWED TO HOLE FIRST.

12. COURSE ETIQUETTE DEMANDS THAT NO PLAYER SHALL USE PART OF HIS PARTNERS APPAREL FOR WIPING HIS CLUB AFTER PLAY.

13. MALE MEMBERS ARE NOT ALLOWED TO PARTNER EACH OTHER.

14. THE TOSSING OF CLUBS BY MALE MEMBERS IS STRICTLY FORBIDDEN. THIS PRIVILEGE IS FOR LADY MEMBERS ONLY.

CRICKET

(As explained to a foreign visitor)

You have two sides
- one out in the field and one in.

Each man that's in the side that's in goes out
and when he's out he comes in
and the next man goes in until he's out.

When they are all out the side that's out comes in
and the side that's been in goes out and tries to get
those coming in out.

Sometimes you get men still in and
therefore not out.

When both sides have been in and out
including the not outs

That's the end of the game.

Howzat!

Dear Friend,

This letter was started by women like yourself in the hope of bringing relief to other tired and discontented women. Unlike most chain letters, this one does not cost anything.

Just send a copy of this letter to five of your friends who are equally tired and discontented. Then bundle up your husband or boyfriend and send him to the woman whose name appears at the top of the list. When your name comes to the top of the list you will receive 16,877 men. One of them is bound to be a hell of a lot better than the one you already have.

DO NOT BREAK THE CHAIN.   HAVE FAITH.

One woman who broke the chain got her own husband back.

At the time of this letter a Friend had already received 454 men. They buried her yesterday, but it took the undertakers 34 hours to get the smile off her face.

YOU MUST HAVE FAITH.

Signed : A Friend
'A Liberated Woman'

Aren't you carrying this AIDS thing a bit too far?

THE REV HAROLD KNIGHT.
THE RESCUE MISSION.
195 ELLIOT ROAD, CAMBERWELL GREEN,
CAMBERWELL. LONDON. W1C

Dear

Perhaps you have heard of me and my nationwide campaign, in the cause of temperance. Each year for the past fourteen, I have made a tour of Scotland, England and Wales, and have delivered a series of lectures on the evils of drinking and drugs. On this tour I have been accompanied by a young friend and assistant, by the name of Joseph Powell. Joe a young man of good family and excellent background, is a pathetic example of a life ruined by excessive indulgence in whisky, pot and women.

Joe would appear with me at the lecture and sit on the platform, wheezing and staring at the audience through bleary, bloodshot eyes, sweating profusely, picking his nose, passing wind and making obscene gestures, while I would point him out as an example of what drinking etc. can do to a person.

Last summer, unfortunately, Joe died. A mutual friend has given me your name and address and I wonder if you would care to take Joe's place on my next tour?

Yours in the faith,

Rev Harold Knight
Rescue Mission.

FARTING: DOES AND DON'TS

No.7 in the Flowcharting Guide to Life Series.

An invaluable guide to passing wind at Royal and Diplomatic Garden parties, receptions and investitures

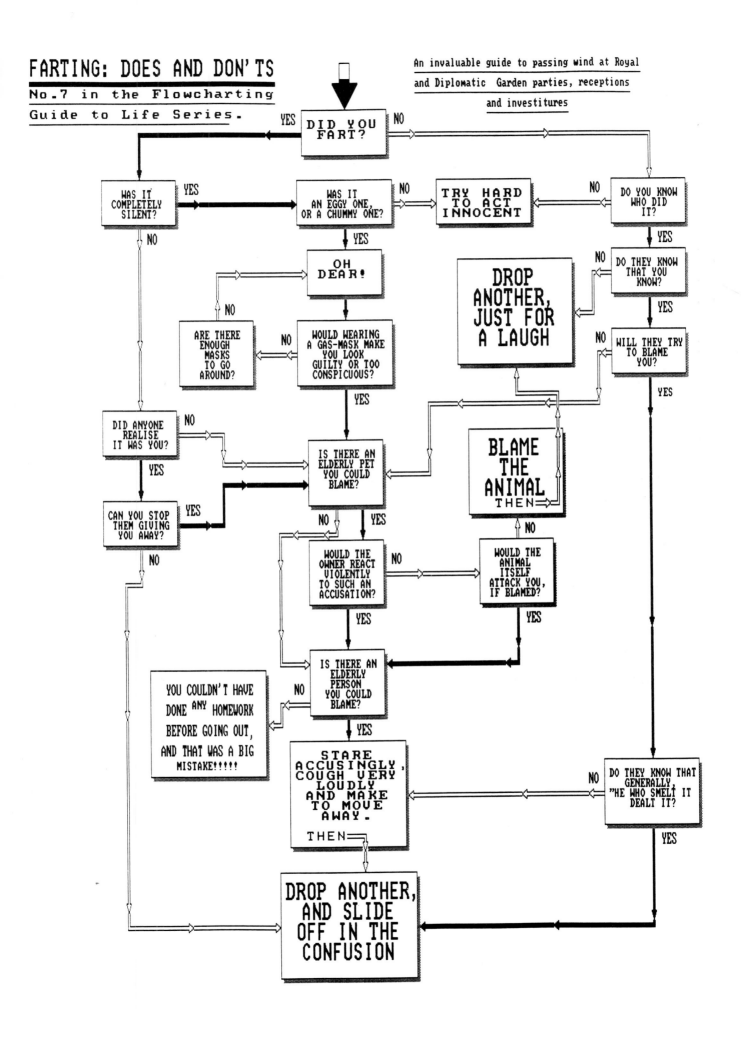

HOW TO KNOW YOU ARE GROWING OLDER

Everything hurts and what doesn't hurt, doesn't work.

The gleam in your eye is from the sun hitting your bifocals.

You feel like the night before, and you haven't been anywhere.

Your little black book contains only the names ending in M.D.

You get winded playing chess.

Your children begin to look middle aged.

You finally reach the top of the ladder and find it leaning against the wrong wall.

You join a health club and don't go.

You begin to outlive enthusiasm

Your mind makes commitments your body can't meet.

You know all the answers, but nobody asks you the questions.

You look forward to a dull evening.

You walk with your head held high trying to get used to your bifocals.

You turn out the light for economic rather than romantic reasons.

You sit in the rocking chair and can't get it going.

Your knees buckle and your belt won't.

You regret all those mistakes resisting temptation.

You're 17 around the neck, 42 around the waist, and 108 round the golf course.

You stop looking forward to your next birthday.

Dialling long distance wears you out.

You're startled the first time you are addressed as oid-timer.

You remember today, that yesterday was your wedding anniversary..

THE PERILS OF FLASHING

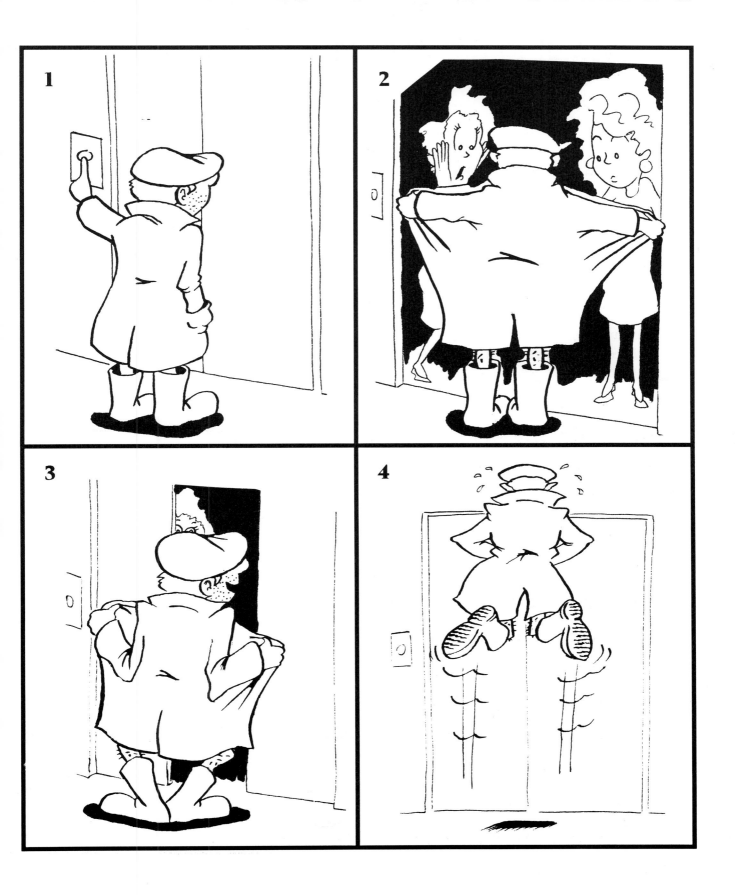

'O' LEVEL EXAMINATION FOR IRISH IMMIGRANTS

TIME ALLOWED   SIX WEEKS

1. What language is spoken by Frenchmen?
2. Give the important characteristics of the Ancient Babylonian Empire with particular reference to Architecture & Literature OR give the first names of the Beatles.
3. What religion is the Pope?
        (a) Jewish   (b) Catholic   (c) Hindu   (d) Anglican   Underline ONE only.
4. What is a silver dollar made of?
5. What is the time when the big hand is on Twelve and the little hand is on One?
6. APPROXIMATELY how many Commandments was Moses given?
7. Spell:
        (a) London   (b) Dublin   (c) Belfast   (d) Guiness
8. What country is the Queen of England queen of?
9. What are the people in the North of England, are they?
        (a) Easteners (b) Southerners (c) Westerners (d) Northerners?
10. Six Kings of England have been called George. The last was George 6.
        Name the other five.
11. Who won World War Two. Who came second?
12. Where does rain come from?
    (a) Supermarkets (b) U.S.A. (c) A big fountain (d) The Sky.
13. Who invented Stephenson's Rocket?
    (a) Winston Churchill (b) Eamonn Andrews (c) Stephenson
14. Can you explain Einstein's theory of relativity?
    YES or NO.
15. What is a coat hanger?
16. Who is buried in Grant's tomb?
17. At what time is "NEWS AT TEN" on?
18. Where is the basement in a three storey building?
19. Explain Le Chatalier's Principle of Dynamic Equilibrium of Forces
    OR write your name in   BLOCK letters.
20. Write the numbers 1 to 10.(Half marks will be allowed if not in sequence).
21. What country lies on the other side of the Irish Channel?
    (a) America (b) England (c) Ireland.

EXAMINATION PAPER 2.
25. Is Eire:
    (a) The stuff you breathe   (b) The stuff on your head,
    (c) A country?
26. Was the Pope's last encyclical:
    (a) A Honda 50 (b) Three wheeler (c) A ban on contraceptives?
    If you have given (b) as the answer to the above question, state whereabouts a male contraceptive is worn:
    (a) On the head (b) On the nose (c) On the foot?

If candidate is Catholic please indicate to which I.R.A. Battalion he belongs and rank held - Bogman or General.
If candidate is Protestant indicate whether Orangeman, Appleman or Leprechaun.

What do they call an Irishman with three 'O'Levels? - A liar.

What does Paddy wear in the summer? - Peep-toes wellies.

What's black and shrivelled and hangs from the ceiling? - An Irish electrician.

What do you do when an Irishman throws a hand grenade at you?
- Pull out the pin and throw it back.

How do you pick out the Irishmen on the oil-rigs? - They're the ones feeding the
helicopters.

How do you confuse an Irishman? - Give him 12 shovels and tell him to take his
pick.

How do you make an Irishman dizzy? - Tell him to piss in the corner of a dustbin.

How do you tell a level-headed Irishman? - He dribbles out of both sides of his
mouth at the same time.

How do you get Paddy to burn his ears? - Phone him when he's ironing.

What do you call a pregnant Irishwoman? - A dope carrier.

How do you tell an Irish Solicitor? - Pin striped donkey jacket and wellies.

Why is urine yellow and semen white? - So that Paddy can tell if he's coming or
going.

Hear about the Irish sea-scout? - His tent sank when camping.

Heard about the Irish parachute? - Opens on impact.

Heard about the Irish Kamakazi pilot? - Completed forty successful missions.

Heard about the Irish Firing-squad? - Formed a circle.

Heard about the Irish nymphomaniac? - Borrowed a vibrator from Wimpey.

Heard about the Irish tap-dancer? - Broke a leg in the sink.

Heard about the Irishman who hijacked a submarine? Asked for £20,000 and two
parachutes. - (Oi'd 'ave arsked for a rowin' boat so Oi would Sorr)

Heard about the Irishman who kidnapped the Irish Prime Minister? - He sent him
 home with a ransom note. They sent him back with the money.

Paddy on University Challenge asked where are the Andes? - Replied on the end of
the wristies.

Asked what was Ghandi's first name replied "Could it be Goosey Goosey?"

Asked what Hippies are replied "Something to hang your leggies on".

How do you define Gross Stupidity? - 144 Irishmen (Why 144)?

Definition of an Irishman - A simple machine that converts Guiness into piss.

Why wasn't Jesus born in Ireland? - They couldn't find 3 wise men and a virgin.

Paddy thought Sherlock Holmes was a block of flats.

Paddy wanted to buy a house. - He went to British Home Stores.

Paddy thought that Ellesmore Port was a type of dinner wine.

Paddy thought Moby Dick was a Venereal Disease.

Paddy thought that Muffin the Mule was a sexual offence.

Paddy's wife gave birth to triplets. He's now looking for the two other men.

AN IRISH MOTHER'S LETTER TO HER SON.

Dear Son,

   Just a line to let you know that I am still alive. I am writing
this letter to you very slowly, as I know that you can't read
fast.

   About your father, he has got a lovely job now, he has 500 men
under him. He is cutting grass in the cemetery.

   You won't know the house when you come home, we have moved.
There was a washing machine in the new house when we moved in, but
it is not working so well. Last week I put 4 shirts in it and
pulled the chain, I haven't seen the shirts since.

   Your sister Mary had a baby this morning, I haven't found out if
it's a boy or a girl, so I don't know if you're an aunt or an
uncle. Last week, your uncle Dick was drowned in a vat of whiskey
in a Dublin distillery. Some of his pals dived in to try to remove
him, but he fought them off bravely. We had him cremated, it took
3 days to put out the fire

   Your father did not drink much at Christmas. I put a bottle of
castor oil in his beer, it kept him going until New Year's Day.

   I went to the Doctor's on Thursday, your father went with me.
The Doctor put a small glass tube in my mouth and told me to keep
my mouth shut tightly for 10 minutes. Your father wanted to buy
the tube from him. It only rained twice last week, the first time
for 3 days and then for 4 days.

   Did you hear the Gale Warnings on the wireless? It was so windy
here on Monday that one of our hens laid the same egg 4 times. We
had a nasty letter from that undertaker who buried you
grandmother, he said that if we do not pay the last installment
within 7 days----up she comes.

   As you said you were feeling the cold on the building site I am
sending your winter overcoat. To save money on postage, I have cut
off those heavy brass buttons, you will find them in the top
pocket.

Your Loving Mother.

P.S. I was going to send you £10 for a Christmas present, but then
I remembered that I had already sealed the envelope..

IRISH SHOWER

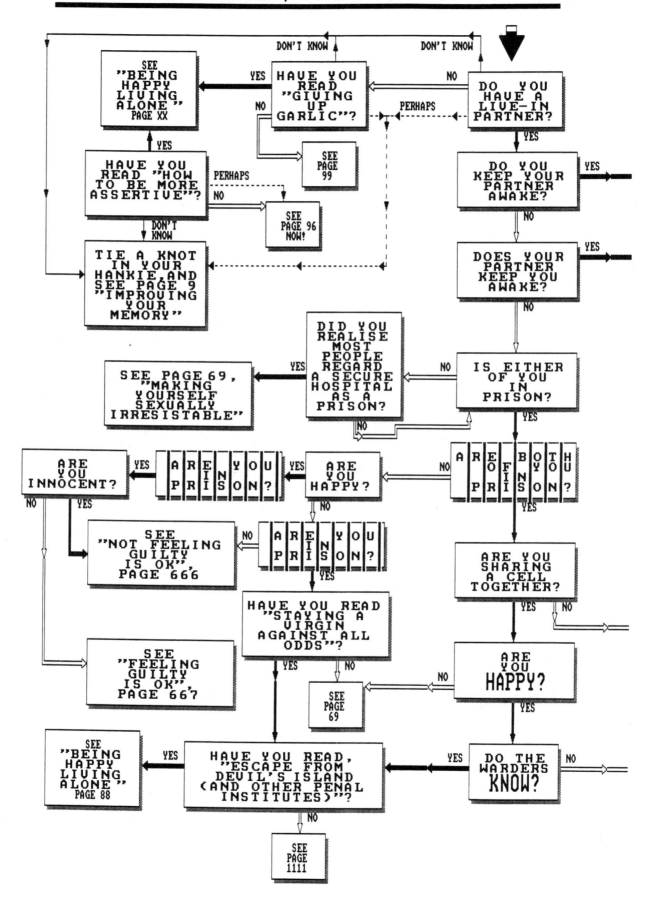

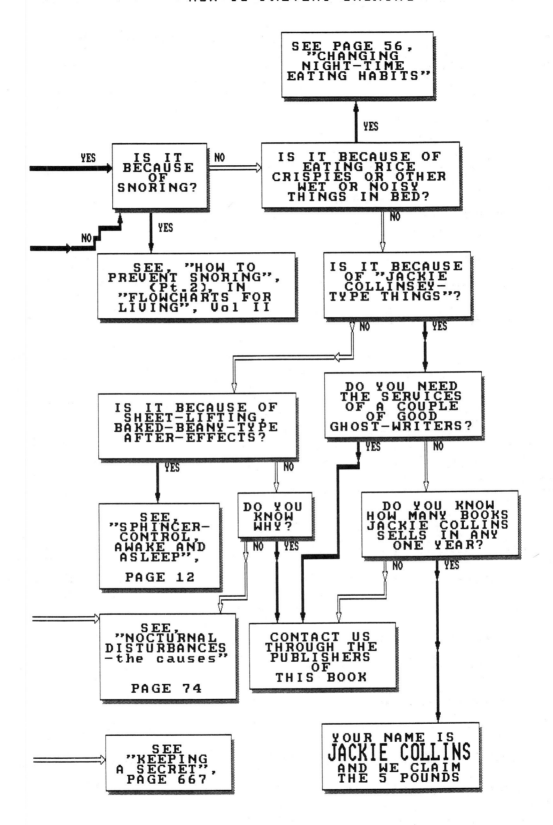

FUNCTIONS OF THE EXECUTIVE

As nearly everyone knows, the executive has practically nothing to do except to decide what is to be done; to tell somebody to do it; to listen why it should not be done, why it should be done by somebody else, or why it should be done in a different way. To follow up to see if the thing has been done; to discover that it has not; to enquire why: to listen to excuses from the person who should have done it; to follow it up again and to see if the thing has been done, only to discover that it has been done incorrectly; to point out how it should have been done; to conclude that as long as it has been done, it may as well be left as it is.

To wonder if it is not the time to get rid of a person who cannot do a thing right; to reflect that he probably has a wife and a large family and that certainly any successor would be just as bad, and maybe worse. To consider how much simpler and better the things would have been if one had done it oneself in the first place, to reflect sadly that one could have done it right in 20 minutes and, as things turned out, one has to spend two days to find out why it has taken three weeks for somebody else to do it wrong.

GENERAL GOODS CORPORATION

An American company sent a shipment of rice to an account in Hamburg, Germany.

En route, mice chewed holes in the bags, nested in the rice and damaged the shipment. The shipping concern, however, sewed up the bags and sent them to the destination. Two weeks late, the American company received the following letter from their account:

Hans Grubeck
Jungfernstem 36
Hamburg
Germany

General Goods Corporation
Green Rice Purchasing Dept
Cotton Exchange Building
New York, N.Y.

Shentlemane,
Der last schipment of rice ve got from you vas with mice schidt gomixt. Der rice vas gut enhoff, but der schidt schpoiled der trade. Ve did not see der mice schidt in der sample you sent us.

It takes too much time to pick der mice schidt durts out from der rice. Ve order kleen rice und you schipt schidt. It vas a mistake, yes, no?

Ve like you to schip us der rice in vun sack und der mice schidt in annudder sack, und den ve gomix to soot der customer. Please write if ve should schip back der schidt und keep der rice, or schip der rice und keep der schidt, or schip back der hole schitten verkes.

Ve vant to do vat is rite in diss matter, ve do not like diss mice schidt business.

Mitt much respeckt.

(signed) Hans Grubeck
Pee Ass: Is der price der same mitt or mittout?

THERE IS ONLY TWO THINGS IN THIS WORLD................

There is only two things in this world to worry about,

Are you going to be rich?

Or are you going to be poor?

If you are going to be rich you won't have anything to worry about.

If you are going to be poor, you only have two things to worry about.

Are you going to be healthy?

Or are you going to be sick?

If you are going to be healthy, you have nothing to worry about.

If you are going to be sick, you only have two things to worry about,

Are you going to live?

Or are you going to die?

If you live you have nothing to worry about.

If you die you will have two things to worry about.

Are you going to go up?

Or are you going to go down?

If you go up you have nothing to worry about.

If you go down, you will have nothing to worry about,

Because all your friends will be there to meet you.

"STRESS"

THE CONFUSION CREATED WHEN ONE'S MIND OVERRIDES THE BODY'S BASIC DESIRE TO CHOKE THE LIVING SHIT OUT OF SOME ASSHOLE WHO DESPERATELY NEEDS IT!

The Meeting

The dogs they had a meeting,
they came from near and far.
Some arrived by aeroplane
and some by motor car.

Before inside the meeting place
they were allowed to look.
Each had to take his arse-ole off
and hang it on a hook.

Now scarcely were they seated.
Each mother, son and sire.
when a dirty little yellow dog,
ran in and shouted FIRE!!!

Now in the rush that followed,
they had not time to look.
And each one grabbed at ransom
an arse-ole off the hook.

The arse-oles all got mixed up,
and they were very sore.
For each dog had an arse-ole
that he had never worn before.

So that is why each dog you see,
will leave a juicy bone.
To smell a dirty arse-ole
in the hope that he'll find his own.

Dear Earthling!

Hi, I am a creature from outer space.

I have transformed myself into this piece of paper.

Right now I am having sex with your fingers.

I know you like it because you are smiling.

Please pass me on to someone else because I'm really horny.

Thanks!

Dear Sir,

I wish to apply for an operation to make me sterile. My reasons are numerous and after being married for seven years and having seven children, I have come to the conclusion that contraceptives are totally useless.

After getting married, I was told to use the "Rhythm Method" but, despite trying the Tango and the Samba, my wife fell pregnant and I ruptured myself doing the Cha Cha Cha; apart from which, where do you get a band from at five o'clock in the morning?

A doctor suggested we use the "Safe Period". At the time we were living with the in-laws and we had to wait three weeks for a safe period when the house was empty - needless to say this didn't work.

A lady of several years experience informed us that if we made love whilst breast feeding we would be alright. It's hardly Newcastle Brown Ale, but I did finish up with a clear skin, silky hair and the wife pregnant.

Another old wives' tale was that if my wife jumped up and down after intercourse it would prevent pregnancy. After the constant breast feeding from my earlier attempt, if my wife jumped up and down she would finish up with two black eyes and eventually knock herself unconscious.

I asked the chemist about the sheath. The chemist demonstrated how easy it was to use, so I bought a packet. My wife fell pregnant again, which doesn't surprise me, as I fail to see how a Durex stretched over the thumb, as the chemist showed me, can prevent babies.

She was then supplied with the coil and, after several unsuccessful attempts to fit is, we realised we had got a left hand thread and my wife is definitely a right hand screw.

The Dutch cap came next. We were very hopeful of this as it did not interfere with our sex life at all but, alas, it gave my wife severe headaches. We were given the largest size available but it was still too tight across her forehead.

Finally we tried the pill. At first it kept falling out, then I realised we were doing it wrong. My wife then started putting it between her knees thus preventing me getting anywhere near her. This did work for a while, until the night she forgot the pill.

You must appreciate my problem. If this operation is unsuccessful I will have to revert to oral sex, although just talking about it can never be a substitute for the real thing.

Yours Faithfully

Mr. 'X'

THE VASECTOMY

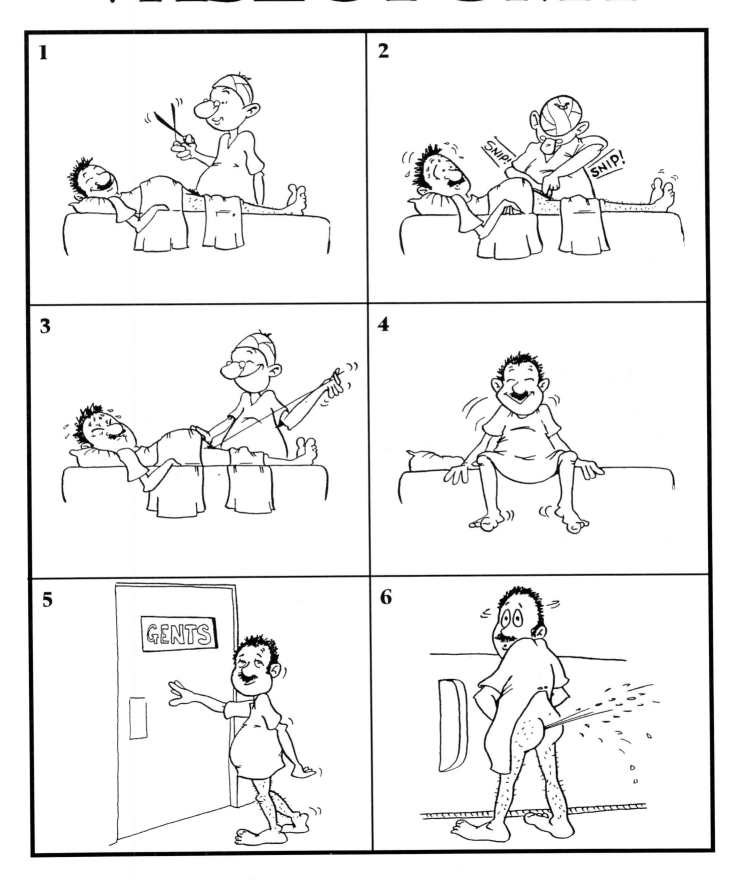

DESIDERATA

GO PLACIDLY AMID THE NOISE AND THE HAST AND REMEMBER WHAT PEACE THERE MAY BE IN SILENCE. AS FAR AS POSSIBLE WITHOUT SURRENDER BE ON GOOD TERMS WITH ALL PERSONS. SPEAK YOUR TERMS QUIETLY AND CLEARLY AND LISTEN TO OTHERS, EVEN THE DULL AND IGNORANT; THEY TOO HAVE THEIR STORY. AVOID LOUD AND AGGRESSIVE PERSONS, THEY ARE VEXATIOUS TO THE SPIRIT. IF YOU COMPARE YOURSELF TO OTHERS YOU MAY BECOME VAIN AND BITTER, FOR ALWAYS THERE WILL BE GREATER AND LESSER PERSONS THAN YOURSELF.

ENJOY YOUR ACHIEVEMENTS AS WELL AS YOUR PLANS. KEEP INTERESTED IN YOUR CAREER HOWEVER HUMBLE; IT IS A REAL POSSESSION IN THE CHANGING FORTUNES OF TIME.

EXERCISE CAUTION IN YOUR BUSINESS AFFAIRS, FOR THE WORLD IS FULL OF TRICKERY, BUT LET THIS NOT BLIND YOU TO WHAT VIRTUE THERE IS; MANY PERSONS STRIVE FOR HIGH IDEALS, AND EVERYWHERE LIFE IS FULL OF HEROISM. BE YOURSELF, ESPECIALLY DO NOT FEIGN AFFECTION. NEITHER BE CYNICAL ABOUT LOVE; FOR IN THE FACE OF ALL ARIDITY AND DISENCHANTMENT IT IS AS PERENNIAL AS THE GRASS. TAKE KINDLY THE COUNSEL OF THE YEARS GRACEFULLY SURRENDERING THE THINGS OF YOUTH.

NURTURE THE STRENGTH OF SPIRIT TO SHIELD YOU IN SUDDEN MISFORTUNE. BUT DO NOT DISTRESS YOURSELF WITH IMAGININGS. MANY FEARS ARE BORN OF FATIGUE AND LONELINESS. BEYOND A WHOLESOME DISCIPLINE, BE GENTLE WITH YOURSELF. YOU ARE A CHILD OF THE UNIVERSE, NO LESS THAN THE TREES AND THE STARS; YOU HAVE A RIGHT TO BE HERE, AND WHETHER OR NOT IT IS CLEAR TO YOU, NO DOUBT THE UNIVERSE IS UNFOLDING AS IT SHOULD.

THEREFORE BE AT PEACE WITH GOD, WHATEVER YOU CONCEIVE HIM TO BE; AND WHATEVER YOUR LABOURS AND ASPIRATIONS, IN THE NOISY CONFUSION OF LIFE. KEEP PEACE WITH YOUR SOUL. WITH ALL ITS SHAMS, DRUDGERY AND BROKEN DREAMS, IT IS STILL A BEAUTIFUL WORLD. BE CHEERFUL. STRIVE TO BE HAPPY.

ANON.

SECRETARY BURNOUT

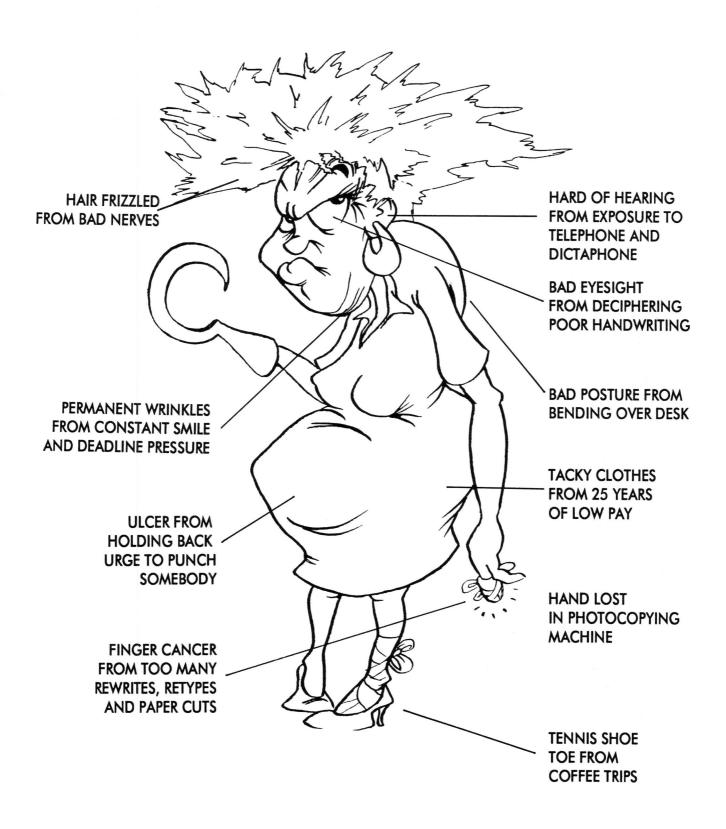

HAIR FRIZZLED
FROM BAD NERVES

HARD OF HEARING
FROM EXPOSURE TO
TELEPHONE AND
DICTAPHONE

BAD EYESIGHT
FROM DECIPHERING
POOR HANDWRITING

BAD POSTURE FROM
BENDING OVER DESK

PERMANENT WRINKLES
FROM CONSTANT SMILE
AND DEADLINE PRESSURE

TACKY CLOTHES
FROM 25 YEARS
OF LOW PAY

ULCER FROM
HOLDING BACK
URGE TO PUNCH
SOMEBODY

HAND LOST
IN PHOTOCOPYING
MACHINE

FINGER CANCER
FROM TOO MANY
REWRITES, RETYPES
AND PAPER CUTS

TENNIS SHOE
TOE FROM
COFFEE TRIPS

THE RULES

The FEMALE always makes The Rules.
The Rules are subject to change at
any time without prior notification.

No MALE can possibly know all The Rules.

If the FEMALE suspects the MALE knows
all The Rules she must immediately
change some or all of The Rules.

The Female is never wrong.

If The FEMALE is wrong it is due to a
misunderstanding which was a direct result of
something the MALE did or said wrong.

The MALE must apologise immediately
for causing said misunderstanding.

The FEMALE may change her mind at any time.

The MALE must never change his mind without
the express consent of the FEMALE.

The FEMALE has every right to
be angry or upset at any time.

The MALE must remain calm at all times, unless
the FEMALE wants him to be angry or upset.

The FEMALE must, under no circumstances,
let the MALE know whether or not she
wants him to be angry and/or upset.

The MALE is expected to mind read at all times.

The MALE who does not abide by The Rules cannot
take the heat, lacks backbone and is a wimp.

Any attempt to document The Rules
could result in bodily harm.

It the FEMALE has PMT all The Rules are null and void.

The FEMALE is ready when she is ready.

The MALE must be ready at all times.

FOR SALE

BY OWNER
COMPLETE SET
ENCYCLOPEDIA
BRITANNICA
EXCELLENT
CONDITION
NO LONGER NEEDED
FUCKING WIFE
KNOWS EVERYTHING

To My Dear Wife,

During the past year I have tried to make love to you 365 times, succeeded 36 times which is an average of once every 10 days. The following is a list of reasons why I did not suceed more often:

1.	We will wake the children	17 times
2.	It's too late	15 times
3.	I'm too tired	25 times
4.	It's too early	52 times
5.	It's too hot	15 times
6.	Pretending to be asleep	49 times
7.	Window open, the neighbours will hear	9 times
8.	Backache	12 times
9.	Headache	26 times
10.	Sunburnt	10 times
11.	Your mother will hear us	6 times
12.	Not in the mood	21 times
13.	Wake the baby	17 times
14.	Watching the late T.V. show	19 times
15.	Too sore	9 times
16.	New hairdo	14 times
17.	Wrong time of the month	4 times
18.	You had to go to the toilet	9 times

During the 36 times I did succeed, the activity was not entirely satisfactory because, 6 times you just lay there, 8 times you reminded me of the crack in the ceiling, 14 times you told me to hurry up and get it over with, 8 times I had to wake you to tell you I had finished and once I was afraid I had hurt you because I felt you move.

Dear Husband,

I think you have got things a little confused. Here are the reasons you did not get more than you did.

1.	Came home drunk and tried to stuff the cat	7 times
2.	Didn't come home at all	29 times
3.	Didn't come	14 times
4.	Came too soon	26 times
5.	Went soft before you got in	18 times
6.	Cramp in toes	9 times
7.	Working late	49 times
8.	You said you had a rash probably from the toilet	21 times
9.	In a fight, somebody kicked you in the balls	4 times
10.	Caught it in the zip	13 times
11.	Got a cold, your nose keeps running	18 times
12.	Brewer's droop	18 times
13.	Your tea was too hot you burnt your tongue	8 times
14.	You had a splinter in your finger	4 times
15.	Lost the notion after thinking about it all day	13 times
16.	Came in your pyjamas while reading a dirty book.	8 times

Of those times we did get together, the reason I lay still was because you missed and was stuffing the sheets. I wasn't talking about the crack in the ceiling, what I said was "Would you prefer it on my back or with me kneeling?"
The times you felt me move was because you had farted and I was trying to breathe. However
6 months ago I phoned Alcoholics Anonymous for their help, and their representative has
been calling most afternoons.

BEER DRINKERS

MAKE BETTER LOVERS

C.O.S.H.H. REGULATIONS 1988

HAZARDOUS MATERIALS DATA SHEET

ANALYSIS	
Element:	Woman
Symbol:	WO_2
Discoverer:	Adam
Atomic Mass:	Accepted as 55 kg. but known to vary from 45 kg to 225 kg.
Occurrence:	Large quantities in urban areas, with trace elements found in most other areas.

PHYSICAL PROPERTIES

1. Surface normally covered in powder and paint film.
2. Boils at nothing, freezes for no apparent reason.
3. Melts if given special treatment.
4. Bitter if used incorrectly.
5. Found in various grades, ranging from virgin material to common ore.

CHEMICAL PROPERTIES

1. Affinity to gold, silver, platinum and all precious stones.
2. Absorbs great quantities of expensive substances.
3. Explodes spontaneously, without warning or reason.
4. Softens and takes on a rosy glow when soaked in hot water.
5. Greatly increased activity when saturated with alcohol.
6. The most powerful money reducing agent known to man.

COMMON USES

1. Highly ornamental - especially in sports cars.
2. Can be a great aid to relaxation.

TESTS

1. Pure specimens turn bright pink when discovered in the natural state.
2. Turns green when placed alongside a superior specimen.

PLAYGIRL

CONSOLIDATED BUILDINGS   regd. office   LONDON
HEAD OFFICE: NEW YORK   PARIS

                                                                        NEW YORK

CENTREFOLD DIVISION

Your name has been submitted to us with your photograph, and I regret to inform you that we will be unable to use your body in our centrefold.

On a scale of 0-10 your body was rated -2 by our panel of women ranging in ages from 60-75 years. We tried to assemble a panel of the age bracket of 25-35 years, but we could not get them to stop laughing long enough to reach a decision.

Should the taste of British women ever change so drastically that bodies such as yours would be appreciated in our centrefold, you will be notified by this office. In the meantime don't call us, we'll call you.

Sympathetically

EDITOR
Playgirl Inc.

P.S. We do commend you for your unusual pose. Were you wounded in the war or do you ride a bike a lot?

BRIGHTON CRICKET

An interesting game took place today when the Hon. John Everard brought over a team of Old Barstodians to meet a team of Society Ladies captained by Lady Wearwell.

The proceeds were augmented by various lotteries but the Chief Constable ordered all draws off.

After tossing was done with, it was seen that the men were going in first and the ladies assumed their proper positions on the ground.

The ladies captain, I noticed, was in the slips, this made it rather difficult to force things.
Mr. Hampton was succeeded at last and cutting and pulling steadily he and Mr. Cox put up a successful stand. The latter appeared to have dug himself in and the blocking steadily resisted all Miss Pratt's efforts to draw him out. Unfortunately, when trying to pull squarely to leg, he completely missed his stroke and out came his middle stump.

Mr. Woodcock followed and was at the crease twenty minutes displaying great patience. There was a sharp appeal from Miss Conduct and the umpire's finger went up.

Some slackness in the field was apparent when Miss Carriage dropped a sitter in front of the pavilion.
Miss Wantcock managed to get her hand to a hard one but failed to hold it.

The men were all out by lunch time.

On resuming, it was noticed that A Testicle was dropped and not merely suspended as rumoured. Lord Faughskin was in his usual position at cover points and the first two ladies, Phil Chambers and Poppy Tupper opened with great confidence. The ladies' captain, Lady Wearwell, used the long handle with great vigour and produced excellent results.
Cox was tired but succeeded in bowling a maiden over. He kept a beautiful length but his balls were inclined to limp a little, much to the ladies' discomfort.
Little Miss Virgo Intacta was loudly cheered when she faced John Everard, but she had no time to settle down comfortably before the wily Everard sent up a long one which seemed to break into her crease, There was an ominous click and a groan was heard as she walked back to the pavilion. There were four more ladies to come and with the rain threatening it looked as though they would have their backs to the walls. Great things were expected of Major Toole, but after he had been at the Nursery End for half an hour they threatened him with great respect and he declined to come off. Although he was keeping his balls low, Miss Ophelia Pratt hooked one, much to the delight of the crowd. There was faulty judgment somewhere. Miss Philpott shouted "I'm coming" and there were cries of "No: and "Wait", but in her excitement she was run out. She said later "Mike Kunt was too quick for me". Miss Hyam Ready then faced the onslaught, but being over anxious she got her leg in front of the straight,and was out. "I had no time to open out" she said later. The match ended in a draw and Lady Wearwell said she would like a return match with the ladies on top for a change.

THE ULTIMATE TORTURE

H.G.V. LORRY DRIVERS HIGHWAY CODE

When should you use head lights? — To warn your mates of a speed trap.

When do you overtake on the left? — When the bastard in front won't move over.

What documents do you take on the road? — Daily Mirror, Sun, Playboy and Forum.

When must you stop? — To have a piss, leg over or a tot of Brandy.

Where should you not park? — Outside the house of the tart you are screwing.

What do you expect to see on a rural road? — Rural tarmac.

How many types of pedestrian crossings are there? — Two - those who do and those who don't.

What is the correct procedure for overtaking on the motorway? — Foot hard down, eyes shut and sweat.

When should you use the fast lane on the motorway? — When you are going home on a promise.

What do you do in the event of a breakdown on a motorway? — Leave the fucking thing and hitch a lift home.

What does a yellow junction box mean? — They have run out of white paint.

What do broken white lines mean on the road? — Careless Navies.

What does the highway code say about tyres? — Use only round ones.

When can you cross double white lines in the road? — After 9 Lagers, 2 Vodkas and a Whiskey.

How do you avoid drowsiness on the motorway? — Finger your hitch-hiker.

What must you check before leaving a building site? — That you have enough timber under the sheet for a new kitchen cabinet.

What do double yellow lines on the side of the road mean? — A Chinese takeaway shop.

Where do you situate your Danger Triangle when broken down? — Up the Transport Manager's arse.

Further copies may be obtained from H.M. Stationery Office Price £1.00

INTERNAL MEMORANDUM

SPECIAL HIGH INTENSITY TRAINING

In order to assure that we continue to produce the highest quality work possible, it will be our policy to keep all employees well trained through our programme of SPECIAL HIGH INTENSITY TRAINING (S.H.I.T.). We are giving our employees more S.H.I.T. than any other office in town.

If you feel that you do not receive your share of S.H.I.T. on the job, please see your supervisor. You will be placed on the top of the S.H.I.T. list for special attention.

All of our supervisors are particularly qualified to see that you get all the S.H.I.T. you can handle at your own speed.

If you consider yourself to be trained enough already, you may be interested in helping us to train others. We can add you to our BASIC UNDERSTANDING LECTURE LIST, SPECIAL HIGH INTENSITY TRAINING (B.U.L.L. S.H.I.T.) programme.

Thank you,

BOSS IN GENERAL
SPECIAL HIGH INTENSITY TRAINING
(B.I.G. S.H.I.T.)

P.S. With the personality some of you display around here, you could easily become the DIRECTOR OF INTENSITY PROGRAMMING
(D.I.P. S.H.I.T.)

All dumb shits who are willing to join this programme, please sign here:

....

....

....

If you have further questions, please address them to our
HEAD OF TRAINING, SPECIAL HIGH INTENSITY TRAINING
(H.O.T. S.H.I.T.) programme.

IRISHMAN'S LETTER TO THE D.H.S.S. IN RESPECT TO RECEIVING AIDS LEAFLET.

Dear Sirs,

I have just received the AIDS leaflet through my door, and would like to apply straight away for AIDS.

I have been on the dole for the past ten years and have been living on supplementary benefit and every other state aid I could get. It now seems I will be getting aid for sex. It's a pity this AIDS has come so late as I have already got 15 children and wondered if you will be paying back payments.

Your leaflet states that the more sex I have the more chances I have of getting AIDS. My only problem here is persuading the wife, who is not so keen after 15 kids. Several years ago I bought some sex aids but she showed little interest and they were hardly used. Would there be any chance of a refund for the £17.50 I paid for these gadgets?

Anyway, I will now explain to her that the government wil lnow be paying us for all the sex we have and I'm sure she will agree that we can't let a chance like this slip by.

You also state that I can pass my AIDS on, but as you will understand with a wife and 15 kids to feed there won't be much left to pass on. If by any chance there is a bit left though I will pass this on to my poor old mother-in-law who has only got her pension.

I understand from your leaflet that I can get AIDS through a blood transfusion and I intend to write to my local hospital straight away to see when I can have one. Will the AIDS I get from the hospital be deducted from the AIDS I get from you? Perhaps you will write and let me know.

I am a firm believer in getting every aid from the country I can get and I'm sure you'll agree that by my past performance I do qualify for this one.

Could you let me know how much I will get paid each time, and will it be weekly or monthly payments?

Yours Faithfully,

Shamus O'Toole

P.S.
Your advert is great, I certainly won't die of ignorance, I know my rights.

S.T.D.
INSTRUCTIONS FOR USING THE NEW DIAL TELEPHONES

On the telephone there is a dial with letters to indicate the exchange required. For instance : S for South, P for Portobello or Pussy, if using the phonetic code and O for Operator.

If the South is required, put your finger in the S hole, if Portobello is required put your finger in the P hole, or Pussy, according to your requirement, and if the O is wanted, put your finger in the Operator's hole and work your finger until she comes and then she will give you the required connection.

If you have fingered the P hole or the Operator's hole correctly you should hear a soft purring sound. Should you have inserted your finger into the wrong hole, the R's hole for instance, you will hear a high pitched scream. In this event, discontinue using your finger and put the end of your pencil in Pussy. When you finish, you may find the Operator has lost her ring.

SPECIAL INSTRUCTIONS.

Foreign calls may be made by dialling the letter F, but the girl may require you to use another letter, usually a French letter, in addition to the normal procedure.

GENERAL INFORMATION

In certain cases satisfactory connection may prove impossible, this could be due to: -

(a) Two or more subscribers fingering the Operators Hole at the same time.

or

(b) The cable engineer having slipped a length in the Operators socket.
    You will then have to wait for service until the Engineer has removed his.

TO REMOVE THE ABOVE FAULTS

(a) Hold the instrument tightly round the middle with you left hand and feel underneath the bottom with your right hand until the Operator responds.

(b) Remove your finger from either the P hole or the R's hole, grasp the flex and pull your wire until you hear a buzzing in your ear.

Safety First Guarantee

THIS IS TO CERTIFY that I, the undersigned, a female about to enjoy intercourse with.. am above the age limit and consent, am in my right mind and not under the influence of any drug or narcotic, neither does he have to use force, threats or promises to influence me.

I am in no fear of him whatsoever, do not expect him or want him to marry me nor I marry him. I do not know whether he is married or not, nor do I care. I am not asleep or drunk, and am entering into this relationship with him because I love it and want it as much as he does and if I am to receive the satisfaction I expect, I am willing to play for an early return engagement

FURTHERMORE I agree never to appear as a witness against him or to prosecute him under the Mann White Slave Act, neither shall I insist that he wears a contraceptive.

Signed before slipping off my panties, this ....

day of................. 19............

Witness........................ Address..

....

COPY OF A LETTER FROM A MELBOURNE GENTLEMAN IN REPLY TO AN INCOME TAX FINAL DEMAND NOTE

Dear Sir,

Your super heated letter arrived this morning in an open envelope with a penny stamp on it, and it would have given the boy and myself much pleasure had it not revived for us a melancholy reflection of what has gone before. You say you thought the account could have been settled long ago and could not understand why it hadn't. Well, here is the reason.

In 1954 I bought a saw-mill on credit. In 1955 I bought a team of horses, a timber wagon, two ponies, a double-barrelled shotgun and two razor backed pigs - all on credit.

In 1956 the bloody mill was burnt down, leaving not a damned thing. One of the ponies died and I lent the other to a stupid bastard who starved the poor bugger to death. Then I joined the Church.

In 1957 my father died and my brother was hanged for raping a pensioner. A tramp seduced my daughter and I had to pay the bastard £50 to stop him becoming one of my relations.

In 1958 my boy got mumps which spread to his balls and the poor lad had to be castrated to save his life. Later I went fishing and the rotten boat overturned, drowning two of my sons, neither of them being the one who was castrated.

In 1959 my wife ran away with a sheep rearer, leaving me with twins as a souvenir. Then I had to have a housekeeper, so I married her to keep the expenses down, but I had a hell of a time to get her pregnant. I went to the doctor and he advised me to create some excitement at the crucial moment. That night I took my shotgun to bed with me. At the time I thought was right, I leaned out of the bed and fired the gun through the window. The wife shit the bed, I ruptured myself and next morning I learnt I had shot my best cow.

In 1960 some rotten bugger cut the nuts off my prize bull. I was buggered and took to drink. I didn't stop until all I had left was a pocket watch and weak bladder. Winding the watch and going for a piss kept me busy for a time. After a year I took heart again and bought on credit a manure spreader, a reaper, a binder and a car.
Then the floods came and washed the bloody lot away.

My wife got V.D. from a travelling salesman and my boy died from wiping his arse on a rabbit skin which was infected. To cap it all some bastard mated my cow to a broken down bull.

It does surprise me when you say you will make trouble if I don't pay up.
If you can think of anything that I have missed I should like to know about it. Trying to get money out of me is like trying to poke butter up a porcupine's arse with a red hot poker.

I am praying for a shower of skunk shit to pass your way and I hope the centre of it is over the bunch of bastards in your office who sent me this demand note.

Yours for more credit,

Robert Arkwright.

THE TWELVE DAYS OF CHRISTMAS

14th December
My Dearest Darling John,
I went to the door today and the postman delivered a Partridge in a Pear Tree.
What a delightful gift. Thank you darling for the lovely thought.
With deep love and affection always,
Your loving Agnes.

15th December
My Dearest John,
Today the postman brought your very sweet Two Turtle Doves. I am delighted,
they are adorable.
All my love forever, Agnes.

16th December
Dearest John,
Oh, how extravagant you are. I really must protest. I don't deserve such generosity.
Three French Hens. I insist you are too kind.
My love Agnes.

17th December
Dear John,
What can I say. Four calling Birds arrived this morning with the postman.
Your kindness is too much.
Love Agnes.

18th December
Dearest John,
What a surprise. Today the postman delivered Five Gold Rings, one for each finger.
You really are an impossible boy, but I love you.
Frankly all the birds are beginning to squawk and are getting on my nerves.
Your Loving Agnes

19th December
Dear John,
When I opened the door this morning there were actually Six bloody great Geese Laying Eggs
all over the front step. What on earth do you think I can do with them all?
The neighbours are beginning to smell them and I cannot sleep. Please STOP sending them.
Agnes.

20th December

John,

What is it with you and these sodding birds? Now I get Seven Swans a Swimming.
Is it some sort of Goddamned Joke? The house is full of bird shit and it is not funny anymore.
Stop sending these bloody birds.

Agnes

21st December

O.K. Buster,

I think I prefer the birds. What the hell am I going to do with Eight Maids-a-Milking?
It's enough with all those bloody birds and now I have eight cows shitting all over the house
and mooing all night.

Lay off Agnes.

22nd December

LOOK CRAPHEAD

What are you? Some kind of nut? Now I have Nine Pipers playing and Christ do they play!!!
When they aren't playing their sodding pipes, they are chasing the maids through the cow shit.
The cows keep mooing and trampling all over the bloody birds and the neighbours are
threatening to have me evicted.

Get Knotted Agnes

23rd December

YOU ROTTEN BASTARD

Now I have Ten Ladies Dancing. How on earth can you call these whores "ladies" is beyond
me. They are pulling the pipers all nightlong, the cow's can't sleep and have diarrhoea.
My living room is a sea of shit and the land lord has just declared the building as unfit for
human habitation.

Piss Off Agnes.

24th December

LISTEN SHITFACE

What with the Eleven Lords Leaping all over the maids and me, I shall never walk again. The
pipers are fighting the lords for crumpet and committing sodomy with the cows. The birds are
all dead and rotting, having been trampled on during the orgy. I hope you are satisfied you
swine.

Your sworn enemy Agnes.

25th December

YOU STINKING LOUSY SHIT

Twelve Drummers have teamed up with the pipers and are making one hell of a bleeding din.
Both lots have begun buggering the lords as well as the cows and Christ know's what's
happened to the milkmaids. They've probably drowned in the cow shit by now. The only way
I"ve saved myself from being screwed to death is by hiding up that sodding pear tree which has
been so well fertilised by shit that it has grown through the bloody roof.

FUCK OFF Agnes

YOU WANT IT WHEN?!!!?

RUSH JOB CALENDAR

MIR	FRI	FRI	FRI	THU	WED	TUE
8	7	6	5	4	3	2
16	14	13	12	11	10	9
23	22	21	20	19	18	17
32	29	28	27	26	25	24
39	38	37	36	35	34	33

1. THIS IS A SPECIAL CALENDAR WHICH HAS BEEN DEVELOPED FOR   HANDLING RUSH JOBS. ALL RUSH JOBS ARE WANTED YESTERDAY. WITH THIS CALENDAR A CLIENT CAN ORDER WORK ON THE 7TH AND HAVE IT DELIVERED ON THE 3RD.

2. EVERYONE WANTS HIS JOB BY FRIDAY SO THERE ARE THREE FRIDAYS IN EVERYWEEK.

3. THERE ARE EIGHT NEW DAYS AT THE END OF THE MONTH FOR THOSE END OF THE MONTH JOBS.

4. THERE IS NO 1ST OF THE MONTH SO THERE CAN'T BE LATE DELIVERY OF END OF THE MONTH JOBS ON THE 1ST.

5. A "BLUE MONDAY" OR " MONDAY MORNING HANGOVER" CAN'T HAPPEN AS ALL MONDAYS HAVE BEEN ELIMINATED.

6. THERE ARE NO BOTHERSOME NON-PRODUCTIVE SATURDAYS AND SUNDAYS, COMPENSATORY LEAVE OR OVERTIME TO WORRY ABOUT.

7. WITH NO 15TH, 30TH OR 31ST, NO "TIME OFF" IS NECESSARY FOR CASHING SALARY CHEQUE EITHER.

8. "MIRDAY" - A SPECIAL DAY EACH WEEK FOR PERFORMING MIRACLES.

So You Want The Day Off

Let's take a look at what your asking.

There are 365 days per year available for work. There are 52 weeks per year in which you already have two days off per week leaving 261 days available for work.

Since you spend 19 hours each day away from work, you have used up 170 days, leaving only 91 days available.

You spend 30 minutes each day on coffee breaks, that accounts for 23 days each year, leaving only 68 days available.

With one hour lunch period each day, you have used up another 46 days, leaving only 22 days available for work.

You normally spend 2 days on sick leave, this leaves only 20 days available for work.

We are off 5 holidays per year, so your available working time is down to 15 days.

We generously give you 14 days vacation per year which leaves only 1 day available for work and I'll be damned if you're going to take that day OFF!!

YOUR STORY HAS
TOUCHED MY HEART

**NEVER BEFORE HAVE I MET ANYONE WITH
MORE TROUBLES THAN YOU HAVE.**

**PLEASE ACCEPT THIS EXPRESSION OF MY
SINCERE SYMPATHY.**

NOW FUCK OFF AND STOP BOTHERING ME.

A DAY IN THE LIFE OF PADDY

Paddy killed sixty-seven woodpeckers before he found out that Cider came from apples.

Paddy drowned trying to bump start his speed-boat.

Paddy died and wanted to be buried at sea.

Eight of his mates drowned trying to dig the grave.

Paddy bought a scarf and took it back to the shop because it was too tight.

Paddy on the 'phone "how long does it take to fly from Heathrow to Dublin?" Air Hostess "Just a minute Sir." Paddy "thanks a lot."

Paddy opened his car door to let the clutch out.

Are my indicators working Paddy? Yes they are. No they're not. Yes they are. No they're not.

Paddy thought that cunnilingus was an Irish Airline.

How do you tell the Irishman in a car-wash?

He's the one on a motor-bike.

Paddy sterilised his cat by boiling it.

An Irish Police Inspector can read and write.

An Irish Police Sergeant can read or write.

An Irish Police Constable knows somebody who can read or write.

Fastest game in an Irish Pub - Pass the parcel.

Irish Airline Captain over P.A. System. "We are now approaching Shannon Airport. Please put your watches back thirty years."

Paddy burned his legs pressing his trousers.

Paddy couldn't walk fast in his wellies so he asked for a pair with a longer piece of string.

When asked "Where does a General keep his armies?" he replied "In his sleevies."

Paddy drove his car into the sea to dip his headlights.

Paddy bought a bag of moth-balls and was upset because he didn't hit one moth.

Paddy bought six bottles of Guinness and poured four down the toilet so that he wouldn't have to get up during the night.

What is written on the bottom of a Guinness bottle? Open other end.

What is written at the top of an Irish Ladder. STOP.

Paddy was hammering nails into the side of the building and was throwing away hundreds. The foreman asked him why and he said that the heads were on the wrong end. "Bloody fool" said the foreman. They're for the other side of the building."

Paddy thought that North Sea Gas only worked when the tide was in. Paddy tried to gas his Mother - in - Law by throwing her in the North Sea.

Paddy put his shirts in the new fangled washing machine, pulled the chain and hasn't seen them since.

Paddy thought that Johnny Cash was the change from a Durex machine.

Paddy thought Ertha Kitt was a gardening sample.

Paddy ironing his curtains kept falling out of the window.

Paddy drove his lorry off Beachy Head to test his air brakes.

Paddy drove in the Indianapolis 5000 and had 32 pit-stops. One for petrol and 32 for directions.

Paddy went to the dentist to have a wisdom tooth put in.

Paddy thought Pontious Pilot worked for Aer Lingus.

Paddy thought that Itchy Fanny was a Japanese motor bike.

Paddy got a pair of water skies for Christmas. He's now looking for a lake that slopes.

Paddy won two prizes on the Generation Game. Two sliding doors and a conveyor belt.

Paddy Found a milk churn in the hedgerow. Thought it was a cows nest.

Paddy, picking his nose, took the lining out of his cap.

Paddy killed himself jumping off the top of an office block after the foreman told him he used to fly in Wellingtons during the war.

Paddy studying Greek Mythology was asked "What is half man, half beast?" He replied "Buffalo Bill."

Paddy entered for two events in the 1976 Olympics. Heading the shot and catching the javelin.

Paddy's wife wanted a coat made of real animal skin. He bought her a donkey jacket.

How do you tell an Irish Father Christmas? Sack full of Easter Eggs.

The Irish have solved the drought problem. They are going to dilute the water.

PARKING VIOLATION

COUNTY

AUTOMOBILE
LICENCE NUMBER

AM
PM

DATE

This is not a ticket, but if it were within my power, you would receive two. Because of you Bull Headed, inconsiderate, feeble attempt at parking, you have taken enough room for a 20 mule team, 2 elephants, 1 goat, and a safari of pygmies from the African interior. The reason for giving you this is so that in the future you may think of someone else, other than yourself. Besides I don't like domineering, egotistical or simple minded drivers and you probably fit into one of these categories.

I sign off wishing you an early transmission failure (on the motorway at about 4.30pm). Also may the fleas of a thousand camels infest your armpits.

WITH MY COMPLIMENTS

PARKING VIOLATION

COUNTY

AUTOMOBILE
LICENCE NUMBER

AM
PM

DATE

This is not a ticket, but if it were within my power, you would receive two. Because of you Bull Headed, inconsiderate, feeble attempt at parking, you have taken enough room for a 20 mule team, 2 elephants, 1 goat, and a safari of pygmies from the African interior. The reason for giving you this is so that in the future you may think of someone else, other than yourself. Besides I don't like domineering, egotistical or simple minded drivers and you probably fit into one of these categories.

I sign off wishing you an early transmission failure (on the motorway at about 4.30pm). Also may the fleas of a thousand camels infest your armpits.

WITH MY COMPLIMENTS

PARKING VIOLATION

COUNTY

AUTOMOBILE
LICENCE NUMBER

AM
PM

DATE

This is not a ticket, but if it were within my power, you would receive two. Because of you Bull Headed, inconsiderate, feeble attempt at parking, you have taken enough room for a 20 mule team, 2 elephants, 1 goat, and a safari of pygmies from the African interior. The reason for giving you this is so that in the future you may think of someone else, other than yourself. Besides I don't like domineering, egotistical or simple minded drivers and you probably fit into one of these categories.

I sign off wishing you an early transmission failure (on the motorway at about 4.30pm). Also may the fleas of a thousand camels infest your armpits.

WITH MY COMPLIMENTS

TITLES AVAILABLE FROM IDEAS UNLIMITED (PUBLISHING)

PLEASE SEND ME (POSTAGE FREE):

☐ copies "100 CHAT UP LINES" ISBN : 1 871964 008 (128 PP A7) @ £1.99

☐ copies "IDIOTS HANDBOOK OF LOVE & SEX ISBN: 1 871964 083 (128 PP A7) @ £1.99

☐ copies "10 GOLDEN RULES OF CHATTING UP" ISBN: 1 871964 091 (128 PP A7) @ £1.99

☐ copies "SIZE ISN'T EVERYTHING" ISBN 871964 121 (80 PP A7 + GIFT) @ £1.99

☐ copies "HOW TO WIN THE NATIONAL LOTTERY" ISBN: 1871964 148 (80 PP A6) @ £1.99

☐ copies "NOT WON THE LOTTERY YET THEN ?" ISBN: 1871964156 (80 PP A6) @ £1.99

☐ copies "SEX Q & A FOR SO-CALLED EXPERTS" ISBN: 1871964 172 (96P A6) @ £1.99

☐ copies "HAVE YOU SEEN THE NOTICE BOARD?" ISBN: 1 871964 105 (80PP A4) @ £3.99

☐ copies "SEEN THE NEW NOTICE BOARD" ISBN: 1 871964 180 (80pp A4) @ £3.99

☐ copies "SPORT FOR THE ELDERLY" ISBN: 1 871964 113 (48PP A5) @ £2.50

☐ copies "BODY LANGUAGE SEX SIGNALS" ISBN: 1 871964 067 (64PP) @ £2.50

☐ copies "THE BEGINNERS GUIDE TO KISSING" ISBN: 1 871964 024 (64PP A5) @ £2.50

☐ copies "TIPS FOR A SUCCESSFUL MARRIAGE" ISBN: 1 871964 032 (64PP A5) @ £2.50

☐ copies "THE JOYS OF FATHERHOOD" ISBN 871964 040 (64PP A5) @ £2.50

☐ copies "OFFICE HANKY PANKY" ISBN: 1 871964 059 (64PP A5) @ £2.50

☐ copies "OF COURSE I LOVE YOU" ISBN: 1 871964 016 (96PP A6) @ £1.99

☐ copies "WELL HUNG" ISBN: 1 871964 075 (96PP A5 Full Colour) @ £2.99

☐ copies "THE 9 SECONDS SEX MACHINE" ISBN: 1 871964 164 (80 PP A7) @ £1.99

I have enclosed a cheque/postal order for £............................. made payable to
Ideas Unlimited (Publishing).

NAME:...

ADDRESS..

....

....

....

COUNTY:...POST CODE..

Fill in the coupon above and send it with your payment to:

Ideas Unlimited (Publishing)
PO Box 125
Portsmouth
Hampshire PO1 4PP

Postage free within the United Kingdom.

If you wish your purchase to be sent directly to someone else (eg: a Birthday/Christmas/Wedding/Valentines gift), simply fill in their name and address in the coupon above and enclose your cheque/postal order, with your personal message or card, if desired We will be pleased to send your gift directly to your chosen recipient..